Talking to Boys

This book is dedicated to T.

"My boy.
My love.

For me, there is no one else left to talk to."

Summer

I.

I thought about walking away from you, going back to my life, the way it was before as if you never existed.

But when I'd write that line the words would blur from tears because I always knew you existed. Long before I found you, I was certain you were out there somewhere.

Could I pretend you don't exist when you've always been there? Should this be easy?

It is no surprise that you would appear with mystery and risk.
Puzzles that I love.

Walking away from you is leaving me. A piece of my soul unsolved.

Yes, every time I thought
about walking away

I'd just move closer.

II.

I tell you to 'Be Safe'
We both know what that means.

Sometimes, if I haven't said it in a while, you will tell me to be safe and I know it means that you are and want me to know.

Then you usually send a new picture and I can tell immediately that you look strong and clear and healthy and beautiful. Or I believe that you do. Convince myself that you are safe.

It is a day to day

hour to hour
minute to minute
obsession

but in those few seconds
there is a sigh of relief and
some peace

III.

"don't leave me"

in the middle of the night I wake up alone my own voice screaming silently

 and you are not alone in a room of beds and walls

 I can't stop the voice inside me screaming

"don't leave me"

"please wake up and don't stop dreaming"

I know if I were there
I would want to hide too
but don't hide
keep your eyes open

don't

stop

breathing

please I am so selfish

I need you here with me
don't go

IV.

Does being saved mean
you finally admit that
it's just been an excuse to
lie?
A reason to retreat
into a place no one can touch
you?
Is it that you believe you
are untouchable or is it that
you don't want touch?
What if your choices are
intentional
that you know how the story
ends before you start to
write it?
And if they don't leave
willingly, you force their
hand like you try to do with
mine when I don't go.
I'm torn, you see

If you are saved,
will it mean you can
give up the twisted mask of
being 'alone'?
this pretense
that you have no arms to hold
you
that no one really cares
if you live or die?
Does being saved mean
you must finally admit
it's all been a game?

Will you?

What if it's not what you're
feeling
if it's not your heart
that's talking
at all?

What if it is a voice
which is not your voice
but lives in you
talks to you
talks for you

I could scream if it would
hear me, scream to scare it
all away. Helpless.
It's just a trap,
a trap to be silenced
rubber ball gag
thick leather strap   cut
out its tongue
you can't do it by yourself
reach out   reach
out   its brave
to stretch   cause I believe

I believe I hear you
in your own voice
clear as a garden bell
crying out for help from
someone crying out for
someone's arms to hold you
I am SOMEONE
someone who you know
was born to hold you.

But I'm torn you see
Is it that I can hear your
voice or is it another voice
in me telling me what I want
to hear what does it mean
what does it really mean?

It's not easy

I was born to do this
unafraid
conquering fears
Now I
play the opposite side
the white light Queen who
dances in and out of hell
who would never miss a lost
soul and moves on easy
hey I wish him well
I am
Fearless as a dove perched on
a lion's head

I know who I am I am not
shaky
(but you have me shaking)
I am born to do this

born to live life free no
fear

no one to tell me what to do
(Fear isn't for 'I love you')

30 second video clip of 1000
tears
and now I won't be saved if
it means living all my fears
Torn between which of us I
choose to save?
In a perfect world but its
not, it's a voice which is
not my voice
but it's in me
talks to me and talks for me
it's a trap needs to be

silenced

rubber ball gag

thick leather strap

to be saved

can you hear me in my own voice?

clear as a garden bell

Crying out for arms which we know…

were born to hold us do I make any sense at all.

(in a perfect world)

we both have a choice

V.

I woke up to rain.
Rain and wind.
I think the rain is perfect.
Here
it is cleaning away the past
so that when the sun comes
out   (which we
know it will)
it will be fresh and clean.

I don't want an umbrella.

I want to feel rain. I need
to be clean too I know
somewhere miles away from me
the rain is going to fall
from your eyes too and just
like here, it's not sad. It

is a clean release
and a chance to grow

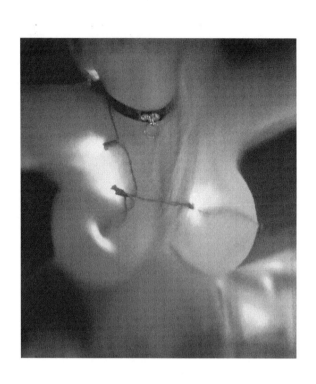

Autumn

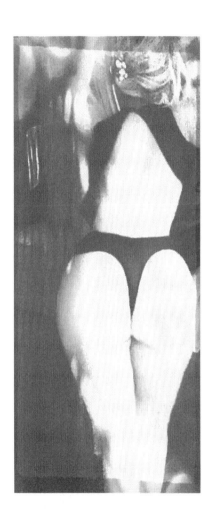

I.

"What was your first thought… after?"

"That you tasted like butterscotch...

"I know. I'm sorry. I thought I grabbed a mint."

"...that you tasted like butterscotch and how much I love butterscotch."

"Oh

 Of course.

Thank you again, Fate."

II.

It's a graceless age when we all follow.

When what you love is based on what you should love as determined by media, friends, family. When your choices are based on anything other than how you feel.

Love survives when you don't let anyone's opinion matter. When you love because it's how you feel and will take the stones thrown at you for that feeling.

Graceless only happens when you condemn anyone else's choice because it makes you that insecure about your own.

III.

I think she loves you
I see it in those eyes
I see it ...
not when she's trippin
from some silly
sweet surprise
you did
no
no that comes not from love
but from some infatuation
could be
for anyone
though it's not...

I think you love her
though logic would defy

'No, I can't really.'
but then you look into her
eyes
or I think
sometimes alone
or
with some other girl
who is not her
you think you do

I hear the thunder
controlled
imagine you want to shake the
earth
I watch you watch her
from opposite sides
as the water flows

between you
waiting for a storm
to change the course of the
stream

I want to tell her
(you want to tell her)
she doesn't need a storm
to change course
she created the stream

when she needed water
and so
she can build a bridge
to get over it
she can do this
we know we have
will she? you hope

I hope too

I think she loves you
I think that
not when she's happy
not when you've done
something
something small
that reminds her what being
happy feels like
I think she loves you
I swear I see it
I see it in those eyes that
flash
fear
like lightening
I see the lightening and know

she's afraid

terrified

of

losing

you

in the storm

before she even

finds you

but

she won't

tell her

(I hear the thunder)
(I see the lightening)

you'll meet her on the bridge
won't you

IV.

You've made me realize
that love is about what you
give and never about what you
get

that life is a gift, no
matter how sad at times,
birds, all animals, wind, the
beach yes even snow is a
gift.

don't hide from it.

and most important, I've
realized that you can know
and understand and love
something you don't always
see or touch.

that's faith that you've
given me   that's
hope, a memory of spirit

V.

You smiled then, a smile for a realist, taking a face of shadow and angles and turning it into a wave of light and movement.

Your lips curled, your eye widened, expectant, pure, so bright to me that I needed to look to the sun on the water for contrast.

You said "Here's a little secret...nothing is real... it's all about who you think you are and where you think you are going."

VI.

You can slice me
watch my blood drip down my
body
and as long as I see that
curled smile and hear your
laugh,
I will laugh with you.
Bloody.
I will roll over for you
to pierce me on all sides of
my body.

This Joker is no joke.

Yes. Do not doubt it.
I am a crazy clown girl.

Intoxicated by extremes.
So it begs for me
to ask that question.

You know the one.
Shhhh.....listen to my
whisper.
"Why so serious?"
Because
and you really need to pay
attention:
I will give it all to
you always
But when it's no longer fun
I give up.

Winter

I.

My church. Small clearing.

Branches tucked away

to open a space to pray.

You might walk by and not even notice.

Snow showers my hair.

In summer I will push through green leaves.

Someday people will visit here.

They will smile thinking of us.

Our voices in this exact spot.

Worshippers of love

II.

this you must know
and remember
you are the one I've listened
to
your voice
your stories
telling big tales
of birds and bugs and rocks
boy things
and I hang onto each word
my questions real
the need to know
to spur your own curiosity
your ability to tell a story
and to remember
someday

your stories
are from another life
the memories of a boy
I will know again
when I hear you tell them
I will listen for the first time
as a child but somewhere
inside me hope I hold
the memory of the
woman I was who would
ask you those questions

III.

I am laying next to you in bed. you are still trying to catch your breath I've recovered mine.

I'm looking around your room at her things pretty little things of no value.

I'm reminded of my tea-cup collection recall finding a perfect little cup in a small boutique that was painted beautifully.
I would always buy it take it home it would never be filled.

it would never serve a
purpose other than a reminder
of something pretty I found
and had to have only because
I could have it

your breath is even with mine
now
I will be leaving
the furtive kisses goodbye
the pattern as familiar as my
teacups
later you will text me
This time
I am home taking each teacup
off the shelf wrapping them
in newspaper
I will look at my phone

though I know it's you
I won't reply
when you text me hours
later...
when you still text me days
months later
I will not reply

IV.

having

never

belonged

to this world

you don't see yourself in

mirrors

you speak without words

breathe without air

I close my eyes

to know you

in the same way

erase the vanity

of wanting to belong

you will never belong

not to anyone

not to me

but still

I can know and say and mean:

hold on to yourself

my love

we are eternal

the facade of human ego

is overrated

we will paint blind pictures

with our cold fingers

in the hot blood we share

V.

Be whoever you want to be.
Love whoever you want to
love. Be with those that
bring you joy. Abandon those
that bring you pain. You
don't owe me or anyone an
explanation.

For taking what wasn't yours,
it became yours so easily.
That is no sin on your soul.
Maybe mine.

Go your own way.
This is your life and no one
else's. You are a unique and

special soul. Ordinary will not know how to love you. But when you find the extraordinary you will know. They will know. They will feel as if no one could have existed on this planet for them before you and this part is so very important, they will feel that no one will ever exist
on this planet for them after you.

Just do not ask me how I know.

VI.

Notice dear my sun shining on
Life is too short to weep
what we can't change is gone
seems like a lifetime in
grief
over what-ifs that didn't
matter   If
you kept coming back to teach
me this to watch as pieces
shatter well enough, done
good this time
lesson finally mastered
not smarter but found my line
push along and forfeit
knowing   that I
burn for you

don't try to see through my
sun shower cause even if it
cuts me through you don't get
the right to break me
you don't get any rights at
all lesson finally mastered
reality builds a wall

VII

I gave you my naked body, but
I was still in Laker's tube
socks.

My 15-year-old naked body.
All hard soft curves.
I bet you didn't even notice
those purple and yellow
socks.

I had no way of knowing I
would never look that good
again. Too young to know what
I was giving you but somehow
even in that innocence unable
to be completely naked

in my best friend's empty house and bed when we should both have been in school.

Instead, it was my first real lesson. Learning how to ride a cock from on top so you could lay back and just watch me, awkward to start but rubbing down on you getting more and more wet, I was such a fast learner. You with those arrogant blue eyes and your cock buried deep inside me, telling me that you could have your cousin 'take care of me' if you moved away. I had said 'After you, no one

will be able to take care of
me'. And it was true for so
many years after. My innocent
words giving you the look of
dominance, proud dominance
that I still hunger for in a
lover. Predator eyes that
have hunted and now know that
they own me.

I hung around for years,
sweet 16, past 17 waiting for
your visits, your long blonde
hair, hunched shoulders, your
10-inch cock in my mouth,
eventually showing me the
tracks on your arms. You were
so proud of those too and I

was so dumb and young then. I was impressed by everything about you as if all I needed to get high was your smell, which even today, writing this, I pause and think because I can remember.

I was yours. Whenever you would show up or call. Asking if I was gonna cream for you. Oh fucking god yes. I would get so lost in it all nothing would stop me.

Until that day in the gay porn trailer in a park south of Po'town. You stood still

as a cat in the window but
you were holding a gun.
Between us a table with a
mountain of cocaine piled
high like in a movie. Leather
and laces that years later I
would learn to love but
seeing for the first time.
Bondage gear and porn photos
under the round red velvet
bed that you fucked me on for
hours. The video camera on a
tripod rolling the whole
time. We were famous.

I was 18 by then but still no
driver's license just a

permit. You had 'borrowed' her mother's car and said you would drive the car back and bring us both home but instead I can picture you as you stood before me in white light, my silhouette behind you, hair a sex mess and my legs still shaky pulling on my panties over thighs that were still sticky and wet with our cum.

You stood there, a Marlboro handing unlit on your lower lip and dangled the keys out to me on one finger without saying a word.

It was like game over crash music playing in my head. I curled up my bra into a ball and just pulled the gauze shirt over my head. I couldn't breathe in there. Red velvet dust in my lungs. Outside I got in her mother's car, behind the wheel feeling scared and afraid but damned if I would show it. I didn't beg you to drive me home. I didn't even ask. I knew what it meant when you pushed that key toward me and I took it

in silence while you were looking at me smug, satisfied with yourself.
A 14-year-old trailer park version of me with a bandana tied around her tits as a top standing next to you with her friends.

I had no lines when it came to you but that day one was drawn. In that minute I leveled up. Grew a little bit smarter on the game. I knew I had given up way too much to you. That one line wasn't nearly enough. It took almost another whole year after. It wasn't that easy. Eventually, weeks, months later I needed to burn all the letters and notes, the cigarette butts I'd saved, the blue satin ribbons and neatly folded little ice packets – burned. Purging started then and for years after I'd gag on my own fingers thinking about your big cock. Heaving up everything inside me trying so desperately to be clean again and get you out of me. It took years to realize what I was doing to myself.

Now I don't think about you much at all except to tell this story. For all I lost to you, that it still takes time to accept, there is one thing I come back to and feel good. I am so proud I left those fucking socks on.

VIII.

You were moving in and out
then. Sometimes sneaking out
of our window
in the middle of the night
not because I would have
fought you but just to avoid
any kind of conversation
about it. You weren't ready
yet to admit it

I knew eventually you would
be going to her for good.
I wanted you to.
I was leaving myself.
I was ready to give up my

pictures of your beautiful
naked body to her long before
she demanded them.

But in the weeks between
Thanksgiving and Christmas,
you

Stayed with me and we started
were playing. The dangerous
way it had all started. You
ended up on top of me with
your hands on my tits. I
watched and then felt you get
hard. We had not had sex
together in months but you
started to pull down my
panties you looked at me for

a second that made me think you would stop but instead you said 'You are gonna get fucked.'

And I did but that's not why I remember this. I remember before we both came you kissed me. We seldom kissed even in the beginning but that night we came with our mouths connected like we were drawing breath from each other and turning into something else entirely. Another entity transforming rising up from the bed in that second-floor apartment with a lock on the bedroom door. We were preparing each other for battle. An exorcism for an evil we didn't even know at that moment existed. Pulling the strength, we would need from each other.

We joked the next morning about peaceful sleep. It had been peaceful, but it was still over.

I was never sure what I meant to you. A good fuck, big tits and a mouth like heaven. That's what you said but after Stephen was gone, at

the house after the funeral,
you gave me my tape back and
said I was the one person who
would never hurt you. Your
eyes looked the same as they
did when I met

you, distant and black like a
storm that is coming. I told
you what a great brother you
had been to Stephen.

We both know we tried. We
were not strong enough. It
was the last time I saw you.

IX.

They smell like summer.
Like seeing your eyes for the
first time and feeling true.
Like the submissive task of
wearing a sundress and
spending a whole day in the
sunshine taking pictures for
you.

They smell like sex. Like
your hard cock pushing
against this thin blue
fabric. Like my pussy
from when I put them on and
rubbed them against my lips

until they were swollen and I could make myself cum so you could watch leaving a deeper blue trail in the seam from all my wetness.

They smell like blood, blood on my fingers, my mouth, my blood, dripping down my thigh. I was high from it. Buzzing. So proud of myself. There are not years of my life that can compare to the ecstasy of those minutes. The ache to show you as strong as the yearning to see you, Master and what you had done.

They are all bits and pieces. Like the reminder of the sweetest boy in a little league picture.
The boy who stood in the snow and lost himself in the pain but somehow is somehow still capable of melting my ice with a dark heart that can be cold as ebony and still melt me, a heart that has had so many reason to give up and give in but doesn't.

They smell strong and sexy and smart.

They are all I've had of you for so very long. Forever.

That is one of the words that
you wrote. Telling me I gave
you the best days of your
life almost as if you knew
then there would be no other
days for us. As if you knew
our plans were just make
believe.

I'm afraid the scent will
fade. The thought of holding
the blue fabric to my face
and not being able to smell
you is terrifying. So, I
decided I will only take them
out on this day. Just for a
minute, one day each year, I
will hold them to my face and

breathe you in only on that one day each year but each year until the day I die and forever on. I will close my eyes. Breathe.
I will close my eyes and hope on that year and that every year that has passed for you since is better than the last. I will hope that the best days of your life only began with me and that even though my heart aches that they didn't continue with me I still hope and will hope every year that you still have more and more best days.

X.

I heard you sold your house and moved away. I didn't hear it from you. By the time I heard it though, I felt nothing.

We survived so much. I thought sitting in that cold unfamiliar office building all those years ago when I put the responsibility of my position over my love for you, I thought then it would be the last time we spoke and then it broke my heart. But

we didn't die then. But it
was like a bad break that
doesn't heal clean. There is
a piece of flesh and bone
that will never come together
like it did before. We could
still move but sometimes it
would hurt.

I don't know what finally did
it. You stopped reaching out,
stopped responding to me when
I reached out and eventually,
I stopped calling out to you
at all. It's like I expected
it would end. Even though it
took longer, it's not

unexpected. It's the way the story was written. As if we feared the touch would destroy us. I guess maybe it would have.

XI.

I think of you in high rise hotels. Room service. 5-star dining. Recall our conversations, imagine you naked, so dark against the pure white sheets. Novice but learning eventually leaving each other behind as we devoured the throngs of groupies that were waiting for us.

I imagine that before too long we will meet in one of those hotels and compare notes.

Spring

I.

I had a dream I was in
Scotland.
It was all beautiful
sunshine.
I woke up and in New York it
was raining.
For days after, all I could
think about was you.
How the littlest things you
do
help me through such a
difficult time. I've never
told you that.
We know without words.

I was connected to you before

I met him. Years before.
But not with red cotton, no
tied with a gossamer thread.
In the first thought,
he reminded me of you.
Do you see a resemblance?
But I came to realize
it was only on cold surfaces.
The fire in your eyes burns
me
like whiskey down my throat
into
my gut swirling there
like in a glass
melting the ice
he left around my heart.

I think about the planes
that cross the sky from my
airport to yours and that I
am still not on them. If I
had gone when I was supposed
to, my path would not have
crossed his in the same
jagged line.

I needed him. You know it.
I would do it again.
I needed those scars.

Yet, I dream about Scotland.
So this is how the story
goes.
And if (when) I touch down,

it will have been sunny in
New York but will most
certainly be raining
there and you won't bring an
umbrella.

II.

I can still remember the way
my hand looked stretched out
on that fake wood countertop
with crumbs from my grocery
store birthday cake premature
Jell-O shot sticky
hiding out in some horror
movie trailer park

the lone witness of my own
fantasy collapse needing a
protection plan, a disguise

I can still remember the way
your hand looked tan, rough
pushing down wrapping around
my fingers feeling warm

pushing down

Later tongues, legs caught in a motion light falling into the woods laughing drunk high all just a blur

(I didn't want memories of anything then)

no one aware but the two of us of the start button under our fingers that we never pushed.

III.

I've known that you
cannot see yourself in
mirrors
I understand that you
cannot see yourself as you
are
only as you were
so feel instead of see
When you think and feel now
doing the same things you
have always returned to
before. Do you feel the same?
What are you thinking?
I know the face twists a
smile. The eyebrows raise.
The fingers click and share

click and share
Mindless habit leads to
mindless habits until the
only thing you will hear is
the sound of blood in veins.
thudthudthudthud
Listen for more
Feel it inside you, deep
inside touch the same place
where your heart used to be
The spot that I touched
I know I did
I'm sure it's still tender
there   Find
it and touch it
Dig your fingers in and hold
on

until you can pull it out
How many lives will you live
without it?

IV.

The truth is and if you are familiar with the story you know:

Persephone is

she is dancing in the garden
in her flowered dress smiling
but blending in
dripping smearing
like a watercolor
And dreaming of a dog
with three heads
and a tight leather collar.
with a choke chain
and the Master who gives up
life   to

rule cold things.
that live below
far below
the roots of her flowers.
It's not about what he wants
or about what her mother
would have wanted for her.
This is her story.
Persephone is lost.
Persephone is selfish.
Which is it?
The world screams:

"Pick a side."

And she looks up from the
pale rose she is smelling

smiles and bites her lip
until the blood drips
down her chin
in a most certain path
an imperfect drop splashing.
onto a petal.

V.

In a fragile moment
she never thought
she'd see the sun again
I tried to turn her around
turn her face to the window,
but she stood limp
didn't care to look

and I can't say for sure,
but I imagine you standing in
front of a window
clouded with dust
refusing too,
to look up at the sky

Yet somehow,
without being able to see

clearly you both began moving
pushing your way toward light
through roots and water
shaking off dirt and pushing
up

I have been in awe
as a gardener grows
watching you
turn her face to light
Collecting water in her hands
as she turned pouring into
you as if from a fountain
with no need for a coin.
You found each other
exactly as you were meant to,
growing in spring grass.

VI.

I climbed over wrought iron
porch rails for you to fuck
me with a big dildo because
your penis was so small.

If I had not been drunk
I would have just hopped back
over the railings to go home
and masturbate but instead
I let you fuck me with that
thing and bite my neck.

In the morning, I went to
work with your teeth marks as
a collar.

Her eyes looked up saw the marks and then looked down. I'm sure she knew they were from you and I felt a little bad about that.

My smile was sympathetic. Something about knowing her secret, sharing her dildo vs. her cock gave me a conscious.

VII.

You gave me a kiss for my 19th birthday on the front seat of my parent's car off road somewhere near waterfalls.

I was the driver and we were both a little drunk
Okay more than a little but that's how we rolled then. We would stop at a frozen lake to slide empty wine bottles out as far as we could. Every drive, every wine bottle bringing us closer to that kiss.

By April and my birthday, the lakes had thawed. The falls were thrashing swollen with melted snow. It was a rush. And you were beautiful.

When I saw you for the first time just months before I thought you looked like Jim Morrison with long tangled brown hair past your shoulders.

You were a baby then. Younger than me but already the teacher.

I was used to the cold. Ice blonde amped snow and

crystal. Instead you were all schnapps and fire and smoking bowls. We would drive around for hours talking of music and life and everything and nothing. Always a little drunk. A little high.

After my birthday, the drive would end with us trying to find a safe place to park. You smelled like sweat and cigarettes, beer, piss. We dressed alike. Levi's. Tshirts. I was not the girl. You were not the boy. We were the same until our clothes came off. We would never call

it sex. We didn't call it
anything at all. It was my
hand down the front of your
Levi's fingering the head of
your cock. It was you taking
my bra off with aching
slowness and then touching
both breasts gently with all
your fingers before your
mouth would take the place of
a finger. I became a girl in
those moments. A woman. Oh
the way you would suck my
nipple. My hands would get
lost in the silk branches of
your hair holding you there
as if you needed my breast to

live.

No sounds but the rush of the waterfall and my moans muffled against the black bench seat of an old Buick. When we would fuck, your mouth would never leave my nipples until you were ready to cum.

I remember hearing you had gotten a new job at a grocery store. I had not seen you in weeks. I'd heard you were in some trouble and I wasn't sure if you were back in jail. When I found out you

were working there I bought a
bottle of cheap vodka and
waited for you in the parking
lot when I knew your shift
was ending. I said I stopped
to show you my new used car,
not my parents, not the big
black bench. You got in and I
remember the stark contrast
of your warm darkness against
the white bucket seats.

I offered you the bottle of
vodka thinking I should have
bought rum but you uncapped
it and took a sip handing it
back to me. You didn't make

small talk. You told me you
had signed up for the
military and were leaving in
a few weeks.

The bottle was raised to my
lips but it slipped from my
hand and you caught it but
not before it had spilled a
little on my shirt. I rubbed
my shirt with my hand and
made light of it. Taking the
bottle from you firmly now.
Throwing back a big swallow.
I said how the military
sounded exciting. My fingers
rubbed the wet spot on my

shirt. You watched me with the solemn eyes of a soldier letting a comrade die. You didn't kiss me goodbye.

I drove home fast and numb. Later inside, I was getting undressed in front of my mirror. I didn't cry until that moment seeing there was a wet spot on my bra right near the nipple, as if milk had leaked through.

VIII.

I was playing with girls then
but that's a long story of
it's own. Although I'd known
how fine you were before,
that night you stood before
me in the woods in tights and
eyeliner, a medieval
Chippendale.
I wanted to strip you myself
Pagan style and ride your
cock like a sword cutting me
open as a sacrifice to the
gods that bring women back
safely from the isle of
lesbos.

I didn't though. I didn't even hint to what I was thinking. Instead I waited until years later in a Vegas hotel room when the gods rescued me I took off my heels and all my clothes and showed you the body that I'd hidden under that peasant cloak.

Even now years later I don't know what keeps me from you. As if the roles we played that night keep our classes separate. Taboo.

Oh but those eyes rimmed in black. I think I learned in that moment looking in those eyes that we don't need to pick a religion or a class or a sex. You were a Knight who didn't rescue me, but you did help me save myself.

IX.

Somewhere in between the sobbing sadness, which was just my selfishness, blaming you for not waiting for me and in between blocking and unblocking and crying and refusing to cry, I realized we, you and I are not of the Earth.

I realized what we have is fireworks in the sky, oh so brilliant streaks of color and light exploding like, yes just like, supernovas in our brains.

We are binary stars orbiting each other surviving with

each other but moving in
paths that do not cross and
it's not my fault and I've
realized it's not yours
either. It is not one of
those connections that people
make up that require constant
physical closeness, instead
we are as the Moon and the
Sun.

Feeling how it can pull with
just the thoughts of you and
that with your words I can
get as wet as the ocean. I
can explode in the sky in a
million colors and every day
is 4th of July. That is our
sky. In our universe it is
eternal summer, hot, sweaty,
playtime with only as much
responsibility as school

recess allows. There are no newspapers to share our picture. I keep my name.

I have come to accept this. I fell in love with your light knowing now why you did not wait.

The wait would have been in vain. There is too much life for us to live too much stardust. We couldn't wait. We keep moving. It's what we do.

We don't break orbit.

X.

Talking to boys is not fun
anymore.
The realization just
emphasizes your importance.
Oh how I loved it, though,
words whispered, words
implied,
the art
the game of it,
such a big part of me.

Now though,
there is you.
I can sit in silence and be
happy to just think about the
sound of your voice.
I admit I would trade all

words spoken to me
and all words I have said
to hear only that one voice,
to talk only to one boy,
our words together
blurring merging
soft and sexy
as French kisses
but clear as twin bells.

I would trade all the talk
that came before too.
I would bottle it up and send
it away. I would erase it
from memory just to hold the
sound of us in a sacred
space.
You.

My boy.
My love.

For me, there is no one else
left to talk to.
'when I fall in love it will
be forever'
I know what love sounds like.
I know what I sound like.
In my words to you,
I heard my own voice
for the very first time.

Author Notes

I have begun work on my next project which is especially exciting!

In the next version of Talking to Boys, I am asking for your submissions – conversations you had or wished you'd had with people in your life, men and women.

For more information and how to submit your conversation, follow me on Instagram Bethann0415 or Facebook @persephonedistorted.

Made in the USA
Middletown, DE
21 December 2019